Contents

Getting the Most
from LifeBuilder Bible Studies

Many of us long to fill our minds and our lives with Scripture. We desire to be transformed by its message. LifeBuilder Bible Studies are designed to be an exciting, thought-provoking and challenging way to do just that. Their ultimate goal is to help us build our lives on God's Word.

How They Work

LifeBuilder Bible Studies have a number of distinctive features. Perhaps the most important is that they are *inductive* rather than *deductive*. In other words, they lead us to *discover* what the Bible says rather than simply *telling* us what it says.

They are also thought provoking. They help us to think about the meaning of the passage so that we can truly understand what the author is saying. The questions require more than one-word answers.

The studies are personal. Questions expose us to the promises, assurances, exhortations and challenges of God's Word. They are designed to allow the Scriptures to renew our minds so that we can be transformed by the Spirit of God. This is the ultimate goal of all Bible study.

The studies are versatile. They are designed for student, neighborhood and church groups. They are also effective for individual study.

How They're Put Together

LifeBuilder Bible Studies also have a distinctive format. Each study need take no more than forty-five minutes in a group setting or thirty minutes in personal study—unless you choose to take more time.

The studies can be used within a quarter system in a church and fit well in a semester or trimester system on a college campus. If a guide has more than thirteen studies, it is divided into two or occasionally three parts of approximately twelve studies each.

LifeBuilder Bible Studies use a workbook format. Space is provided for writing answers to each question. This is ideal for personal study and allows group members to prepare in advance for the discussion.

The studies also contain leader's notes. They show how to lead a group discussion, provide additional background information on certain questions, give helpful tips on group dynamics and suggest ways to deal with problems which may arise during the discussion. With such helps, someone with little or no experience can lead an effective study.

Suggestions for Individual Study

1. As you begin each study, pray that God will help you to understand and apply the passage to your life.

2. Read and reread the assigned Bible passage to familiarize yourself with what the author is saying. In the case of book studies, you may want to read through the entire book prior to the first study. This will give you a helpful overview of its contents.

3. A good modern translation of the Bible, rather than the King James Version or a paraphrase, will give you the most help. The New International Version, the New American Standard Bible and the Revised Standard Version are all recommended. However, the questions in this guide are based on the New International Version.

4. Write your answers in the space provided in the study guide. This will help you to express your understanding of the passage clearly.

5. It might be good to have a Bible dictionary handy. Use it to look up any unfamiliar words, names or places.

Suggestions for Group Study

1. Come to the study prepared. Follow the suggestions for individual study mentioned above. You will find that careful preparation will greatly enrich your time spent in group discussion.

2. Be willing to participate in the discussion. The leader of your group will not be lecturing. Instead, he or she will be encouraging the members of the group to discuss what they have learned from the passage. The leader will be asking the questions that are found in this guide. Plan to share what God has taught you in your individual study.

3. Stick to the passage being studied. Your answers should be based on the verses which are the focus of the discussion and not on outside authorities such as commentaries or speakers. This guide deliberately avoids jumping from book to book or passage to passage. Each study focuses on only one

passage. Book studies are generally designed to lead you through the book in the order in which it was written. This will help you follow the author's argument.

4. Be sensitive to the other members of the group. Listen attentively when they share what they have learned. You may be surprised by their insights! Link what you say to the comments of others so the group stays on the topic. Also, be affirming whenever you can. This will encourage some of the more hesitant members of the group to participate.

5. Be careful not to dominate the discussion. We are sometimes so eager to share what we have learned that we leave too little opportunity for others to respond. By all means participate! But allow others to also.

6. Expect God to teach you through the passage being discussed and through the other members of the group. Pray that you will have an enjoyable and profitable time together.

7. If you are the discussion leader, you will find additional suggestions and helpful ideas for each study in the leader's notes. These are found at the back of the guide.

Introducing the Sermon on the Mount

The Sermon on the Mount is probably the best-known part of the teaching of Jesus, though arguably it is the least understood, and certainly it is the least obeyed. It is the nearest thing to a manifesto that he ever uttered, for it is his own description of what he wanted his followers to be and to do.

The Sermon is found in Matthew's Gospel toward the beginning of Jesus' public ministry. Immediately after his baptism and temptation he had begun to announce the good news that the kingdom of God, long promised in the Old Testament era, was now on the threshold. He himself had come to inaugurate it. With him the new age had dawned, and the rule of God had broken into history. "Repent," he cried, "for the kingdom of heaven in near" (Mt 4:17). Indeed, "Jesus went throughout Galilee, teaching in their synagogues, preaching the good news of the kingdom" (Mt 4:23). The Sermon on the Mount, then, is to be seen in this context. It portrays the repentance *(metanoia,* the complete change of mind) and the righteousness which belong to the kingdom. That is, it describes what human life and human community look like when they come under the gracious rule of God.

And what do they look like? Different! Jesus emphasized that his true followers, the citizens of God's kingdom, were to be entirely different from others. They were not to take their cue from the people around them, but from him, and so prove to be genuine children of their heavenly Father.

To me the key text of the Sermon on the Mount is Matthew 6:8: "Do

not be like them." It is immediately reminiscent of God's word to
Israel in Leviticus 18:3: "You must not do as they do." It is the same
call to be different. And right through the Sermon on the Mount this
theme is elaborated. Their character (the beatitudes) was to be completely distinct from that admired by the world. They were to shine like
lights in the prevailing darkness. Their righteousness was to exceed
that of the scribes and Pharisees, both in ethical behavior and in religious devotion, while their love was to be greater and their ambition
nobler than those of their pagan neighbors.

There is no single paragraph of the Sermon on the Mount in which
this contrast between Christian and non-Christian standards is not
drawn. It is the underlying and uniting theme of the Sermon; everything else is a variation of it. Sometimes it is the Gentiles or pagan
nations with whom Jesus contrasts his followers. At other times he
contrasts them with Jews.

At all times Jesus teaches his followers are to be different— different
from both the nominal church and the secular world, different from
both the religious and the irreligious. The Sermon on the Mount is the
most complete delineation anywhere in the New Testament of the
Christian counterculture. Here is a Christian value system, ethical standard, religious devotion, attitude to money, ambition, lifestyle and
network of relationships—all of which are totally at variance with those
of the non-Christian world. The Sermon presents life in the kingdom
of God, a fully human life indeed but lived out under the divine rule.

Perhaps a majority of readers and commentators, looking the reality
of human perversity in the face, have declared the standards of the
Sermon on the Mount to be unattainable. Its ideals are noble but
unpractical, they say, attractive to imagine but impossible to fulfill. At
the opposite extreme are those superficial souls who glibly assert that
the Sermon expresses ethical standards which are self-evidently true,
common to all religions and easy to follow. "I live by the Sermon on
the Mount," they say.

The truth lies in neither extreme position. For the standards of the
Sermon are neither readily attainable by everyone, nor totally unattain-

able by anyone. To put them beyond anybody's reach is to ignore the purpose of Christ's Sermon; to put them within everybody's is to ignore the reality of our sin. They are attainable all right, but only by those who have experienced the new birth which Jesus told Nicodemus was the indispensable condition of seeing and entering God's kingdom. For the righteousness he described in the Sermon is an inner righteousness. Although it manifests itself outwardly and visibly in words, deeds and relationships, yet it remains essentially a righteousness of the heart.

Only a belief in the necessity and the possibility of a new birth can keep us from reading the Sermon on the Mount with either foolish optimism or hopeless despair. Jesus spoke the Sermon to those who were already his disciples and thereby also the citizens of God's kingdom and children of God's family. The high standards he set are appropriate only to such. We do not, indeed could not, achieve this privileged status by attaining Christ's standards. Rather by attaining his standards, or at least approximating them, we give evidence of what by God's free grace and gift we already are.

This LifeGuide Bible Study draws on material first published in *The Message of the Sermon on the Mount,* a volume I have written in The Bible Speaks Today series (IVP). I recommend that book as supplementary reading for those using this guide. I am grateful to Jack Kuhatschek, Bible study editor of InterVarsity Press, for the trouble he has taken and the skill he has shown in preparing this guide under my general direction.

Those who first heard the Sermon on the Mount were astonished. I pray that you too will be astonished and challenged by the greatest sermon ever preached.

John R. W. Stott

1
A Christian's Character (Part 1)

Matthew 5:1-12

Everybody who has ever heard of Jesus of Nazareth, and knows anything at all of his teaching, must surely be familiar with the beatitudes. Their simplicity of word and profundity of thought have attracted each fresh generation of Christians, and many others besides. The more we explore their implications, the more seems to remain unexplored. Their wealth is inexhaustible. We cannot plumb their depths. Truly, "we are near heaven here."

1. What types of people do we normally consider blessed or fortunate?

2. Read Matthew 5:1-12. How does our normal description of the blessed or fortunate person compare with those whom Jesus considers blessed (vv. 1-12)?

3. To be "poor in spirit" (v. 3) is to acknowledge our spiritual poverty, our bankruptcy before God. Why is this an indispensable condition for receiving the kingdom of heaven?

Why is it so difficult for us to admit our spiritual poverty?

4. Why would those who are poor in spirit feel a need to mourn (v. 4)?

5. Those who mourn feel sorrow not only for their own sin but also for the sin they see around them. What have you heard in the news lately that causes you to mourn?

6. How do you think those who mourn will be comforted (v. 4)?

7. How would a true estimate of ourselves (vv. 3-4) lead us to be "meek"—to have a humble and gentle attitude to others (v. 5)?

8. From the world's point of view, why is it surprising that the meek will inherit the earth?

9. What has Jesus said so far that might lead us to hunger and thirst for righteousness (v. 6)?

10. Biblical righteousness has three aspects: legal, moral and social. What does it mean to hunger and thirst for each of these?

11. Jesus promises that those who hunger and thirst for righteousness will be filled (v. 6). What can you do to cultivate a healthy, hearty spiritual appetite?

12. Ask God to satisfy some of your hunger and thirst as you study the Sermon on the Mount.

2
A Christian's Character (Part 2)

Matthew 5:1-12

The beatitudes set forth the balanced and multifaceted character of Christians. These are not eight separate and distinct groups of disciples, some of whom are meek, while others are merciful and yet others are called to endure persecution. They are rather eight qualities of the same group, who at one and the same time are meek and merciful, poor in spirit and pure in heart.

Further, the group exhibiting these marks is not an elitist set, a small spiritual aristocracy remote from common Christians. On the contrary, the beatitudes are Christ's own specification of what every Christian ought to be. All of these qualities are to characterize all his followers. They describe his ideal for us as citizens of God's kingdom.

---

1. Why do you think the beatitudes have such universal appeal?

---

2. Read Matthew 5:1-12. How would you define *mercy* (v. 7)?

3. Jesus says the merciful will be shown mercy (v. 7). Why do you think our treatment of others will affect God's treatment of us?

4. What opportunities has God given you to show mercy to those in need?

5. The "pure in heart" (v. 8) are not just inwardly pure, they are "utterly sincere" (J. B. Phillips). Their whole life, public and private, is transparent before God and others. Why is it difficult to live this way?

6. Why would the promise of seeing God (v. 8) be reserved for those who are pure in heart?

7. Why is it fitting that "the peacemakers" will be called sons of God (v. 9)?

8. How can we be peacemakers (v. 9) in our homes, in our churches and in society?

9. How is being a peacemaker different from settling for "peace at any price"?

10. In spite of our efforts at peacemaking, what does Jesus say we will experience (vv. 10-12)?

Why should this cause us to rejoice?

11. Why would the world hate the kind of people described in the beatitudes?

12. Dietrich Bonhoeffer, who was killed by the Nazis because of his faith, wrote: "With every beatitude the gulf is widened between the disciples and the people." How have the beatitudes challenged you to be different?

3
A Christian's Influence

Matthew 5:13-16 Mark 9. 50
Luke 14. 34-35

W hat possible influence could the people described in the beatitudes exert in this hard, tough world? What lasting good can the poor and the meek do, the mourners and the merciful—those who seek peace and not war? Would they not be overwhelmed by the flood tide of evil? What can they accomplish—whose only passion is righteousness, and whose only weapon is purity of heart? Are not such people too feeble to achieve anything? Jesus does not share this skepticism, as this passage demonstrates. He expects us to have a profound influence on those around us.

1. In what ways have Christians had a positive influence on society?

2. Read Matthew 5:13-16. Before refrigeration, salt was used to keep meat from rotting. What then does Jesus' statement "You are the salt of the earth" (v. 13) tell us about society and the church's role in it?

3. What has been in the news lately that indicates society is rotting and decaying?

4. What are some practical ways we can function as salt where we live and work (v. 13)?

5. What might cause Christians to lose their saltiness (v. 13)?

6. Jesus' second statement is "You are the light of the world" (v. 14). As salt we prevent decay, the spread of evil. How does the church's role as light complement its role as salt?

7. How can we positively promote the spread of truth in the world?

8. Why might we be tempted to hide our light (v. 15)?

9. What is the result, according to Jesus, of people seeing our good deeds (v. 16)?

10. What examples can you think of where the work of Christians has brought people closer to God?

11. What relationship do you see between the beatitudes and our role as salt and light in society?

12. What is one way you can begin having a stronger influence as salt and as light?

4
A Christian's Righteousness:
Christ, the Christian & the Law

Matthew 5:17-20

So far Jesus has spoken of the character of Christians. He has also emphasized the influence we will have in the world if we exhibit this character and if our character bears fruit in "good deeds." In Matthew 5:17-20 he proceeds to define further this character and these good deeds in terms of righteousness. This passage is of great importance not only for its definition of Christian righteousness but also for the light it throws on the relation between the New Testament and the Old Testament, between the gospel and the law.

1. In your opinion, what are some of the benefits and difficulties of reading the Old Testament?

2. Read Matthew 5:17-20. This passage naturally divides into two parts, verses 17-18 and verses 19-20. What does each part emphasize?

3. Why might some people have thought that Jesus came to abolish the Law and the Prophets (v. 17)?

4. The Law and the Prophets (the Old Testament) consist of doctrine, prophecy and ethical precepts. In what sense has Jesus fulfilled each of these (v. 17)?

5. How does Jesus emphasize his high view of Old Testament Scripture (vv. 17-18)?

How can Jesus' words strengthen our confidence in Scripture?

6. How will our response to the Law determine our status in the kingdom of heaven (v. 19)?

7. The Pharisees and teachers of the law were zealous about observing the Law. How can our righteousness possibly surpass theirs (v. 20)?

8. Jesus states that only those who have this surpassing righteousness will enter the kingdom of heaven (v. 20). How can this be harmonized with his statement about the poor in spirit (those who admit their spiritual bankruptcy) entering the kingdom (5:3)?

9. Some people claim that Jesus abolished the category of law for the Christian and that we are only responsible for obeying the "law of love." Respond to this view in light of Jesus' words in this passage.

10. How has this passage affected your attitude toward the Old Testament?

11. How can you make your study and application of the Old Testament a higher priority?

5
A Christian's Righteousness
Avoiding Anger & Lust

Matthew 5:21-30

The scribes and Pharisees calculated that the law contained 248 commandments and 365 prohibitions. But they were better at arithmetic than obedience. So they tried to make the law's demands less demanding and the law's permissions more permissive. Throughout the Sermon on the Mount, Jesus seeks to reverse this tendency. He came to deepen not destroy the law's demands. In this passage he explains the true meaning of the sixth and seventh commandments, the prohibitions against murder and adultery.

---

1. Have you ever slowed down your car because you saw a police officer? What did your action indicate about your attitude toward the law?

---

2. Read Matthew 5:21-30. The NIV translates the sixth commandment as "Do not murder" rather than "Do not kill." Why is this an important distinction?

3. In verses 21-22 Jesus places murder and unrighteous anger in the same category. How are they related?

4. A. B. Bruce writes: *"Raca* expresses contempt for a man's head = you stupid!; *[fool]* expresses contempt for his heart and character = you scoundrel!" Why do you think these thoughts and words would be murder in God's sight (v. 22)?

5. What do verses 23-26 teach us about broken relationships?

When we have offended someone, why is it so important that we go to him or her *immediately?*

6. What, according to Jesus, is the full meaning of the seventh commandment: "Do not commit adultery" (vv. 27-28)?

7. Some Christians have taken verses 29-30 literally and have mutilated their bodies. How do you think Jesus intends us to understand his warnings?

8. In what situations might we need to "gouge out an eye" or "cut off a hand"?

How might this spiritual surgery differ from person to person?

9. Throughout this passage, how has Jesus challenged a superficial view of righteousness?

10. In what specific areas do you feel the need for a deeper righteousness?

11. Ask God to help you rid your life of anything that causes you to sin. Pray that you will be able to obey him in your attitudes as well as your actions.

6
A Christian's Righteousness:
In Marriage & Speech
Matthew 5:31-37; 19:3-9

Divorce is a controversial and complex subject which touches people's emotions at a deep level. There is almost no unhappiness so painful as that of an unhappy marriage. And there is almost no tragedy so great as when a relationship God meant for love and fulfillment degenerates into a nonrelationship of bitterness, discord and despair. Yet in spite of the painfulness of the subject, I am convinced that the teaching of Jesus on this and every subject is good—intrinsically good for individuals and for society. In this passage Jesus calls us to faithfulness in marriage and honesty in speech.

---

1. Why do you think divorce is such a problem today?

---

2. Read Matthew 5:31-32 and 19:3-9. Rabbi Shammai taught that divorce was permitted only in extreme cases. Rabbi Hillel taught that it was permitted for any and every reason. How does this help us to understand the Pharisees' "test" question (19:3)?

3. How does Jesus' reply contrast with the Pharisees' question (vv. 4-6)?

4. Jesus points back to the first marriage in Genesis. What does it teach us about God's original design for marriage (vv. 4-6)?

5. The Pharisees refer to Moses' instructions about divorce as a "command" (v. 7). What does Jesus' reply teach us about divorce (v. 8)?

In what ways might divorce reveal the hardness of our hearts?

6. What similarities and differences are there between 19:9 and 5:31-32?

How do these verses stress the seriousness of divorce?

7. How does Jesus' teaching contrast with today's views on marriage and divorce?

8. Read Matthew 5:33-37. How might the issue of oaths and vows be connected to the topic of marriage and divorce?

9. The Pharisees had elaborate formulas for oaths, with some being binding and some not (see Mt 23:16-22). Why is Jesus opposed to oaths?

10. Does this mean, for example, that we should refuse to give evidence under oath in a court of law? Explain.

11. Why should oaths be unnecessary for Jesus' followers?

12. Ask God to help you resist the pressures to compromise in marriage and in speech.

7
A Christian's Righteousness:
Loving Our Enemies

Matthew 5:38-48

This passage brings us to the highest point of the Sermon on the Mount. Christ's words here are both most admired and most resented. He calls us to show our attitude of total love toward an "evil person" (v. 39) and our "enemies" (v. 44). Nowhere is the challenge of the Sermon greater. Nowhere is the distinctness of the Christian counter-culture more obvious. Nowhere is our need of the power of the Holy Spirit (whose first fruit is love) more compelling.

1. A friend keeps borrowing things from you but either fails to return them or returns them damaged. Confrontation has done no good. Do you (a) make the friend pay for anything lost or damaged, (b) refuse to loan anything else to your friend or (c) continue to loan anything he or she asks for? Explain.

2. Read Matthew 5:38-48. Jesus' quotation of "Eye for eye, and tooth for tooth" comes from Exodus 21:24. How would this instruction to Israel's judges clarify the meaning of justice?

How would it also limit the extent of revenge?

3. The Pharisees evidently extended this principle from the law courts (where it belonged) to the realm of personal relationships (where it did not belong). What consequences might have resulted?

4. Looking at verses 39-42, how would you contrast our natural responses in such situations with the responses Jesus expects of us?

5. What is accomplished by turning the other cheek or going a second mile?

6. In what situations might Christ's commands apply today?

7. How can we reconcile Christ's call to nonretaliation with the state's duty to punish evildoers (see Rom 13:1-5)?

8. According to Jesus, how are we to treat our enemies and why (vv. 44-45)?

9. In what ways is Jesus' command extraordinary (vv. 46-48)?

10. Does all this mean that Christians are to be doormats for the world to walk on? Explain.

11. How was Jesus himself an example of the principles "Do not resist an evil person" and "Love your enemies"?

12. How might you reflect your Father's character when you are mistreated?

8
A Christian's Religion

Matthew 6:1-6, 16-18

Not conforming to the world is a familiar New Testament concept. But it is not so well known that Jesus also called us not to conform to the *religious* establishment. He saw (and foresaw) the worldliness of the nominal church and commanded the Christian community to be truly distinct from it in our life and practice. In this passage Jesus shifts his focus from our moral righteousness to our "religious" righteousness.

1. Why do you think ministers and religious people are often portrayed so negatively in movies and on television?

2. Read Matthew 6:1-6, 16-18. In verse 1 Jesus commands us "not to do your 'acts of righteousness' before men, to be seen by them." Yet in 5:16 he said, "Let your light shine before men, so that they may see your good deeds." Is there a contradiction here? Explain.

3. Jesus illustrates the principle of verse 1 by focusing on three religious practices: giving, praying and fasting. What images come to mind when you read about the hypocrites in verse 2?

4. What does Jesus mean when he says, "But when you give to the needy, do not let your left hand know what your right hand is doing" (v. 3)?

Why is this important (vv. 2, 4)?

5. In what ways are we tempted to be hypocritical in our giving?

6. What was wrong with the way hypocrites prayed in Jesus' day (v. 5)?

7. In what ways do hypocrites pray today?

8. Why and how is our praying to be different (v. 6)?

9. How do you think the reward the Father will give us (v. 6) differs from the reward we receive from others (v. 5)?

10. In verse 16 Jesus assumes Christians will fast (although few of us do). Why and how should we fast (vv. 16-18)?

11. In what other areas are we tempted to seek the approval of people rather than of God?

12. How can this passage help to purify our motives?

9
A Christian's Prayer
Matthew 6:7-15

T he fundamental difference between various kinds of prayer is the fundamentally different images of God which lie behind them. The "Lord's Prayer" was given by Jesus as a model of what genuine Christian prayer should be like. According to Matthew he gave it as a pattern to copy ("This is how you should pray"), according to Luke as an actual prayer ("When you pray, say . . ."). We are not obliged to choose, however, for we can both use the prayer as it stands and also model our own praying upon it. Either way, Jesus not only teaches us about prayer but also gives us a greater vision of the God we call "Our Father."

1. Imagine that your prayers, like those in the Psalms, were recorded for others to read. What would people learn about your image of God?

2. Read Matthew 6:7-15. How do pagan prayers (v. 7) differ from the persistent prayers Jesus himself offered (Mt 26:44)?

3. In what ways might we be guilty of mindless, meaningless prayers today?

---

4. If, as Jesus says in verse 8, God already knows what we need, why should Christians pray?

---

5. What two natural divisions do you observe in the Lord's Prayer (vv. 9-13)?

What is the focus of each?

---

6. What does the phrase "Our Father in heaven" (v. 9) tell us about God?

---

7. What does it mean to hallow God's name (v. 9)?

8. God is already King. In what sense are his kingdom and perfect will still future (v. 10)?

9. In our self-centered culture we are often preoccupied with our own little name, empire and will rather than God's. How can we combat this tendency?

10. Some early commentators allegorized the word *bread* (v. 11), assuming that Jesus could not be referring to something as mundane as our physical needs. Why is it perfectly appropriate to pray for actual "daily bread"?

11. How is our heavenly Father's forgiveness related to our forgiving others (vv. 12, 14-15)?

12. If God cannot tempt us and trials are beneficial (Jas 1:2, 13), then what is the meaning of Matthew 6:13?

13. In what ways do your prayers need to more closely resemble this model prayer?

14. Take time now to pray, using the Lord's Prayer as your model.

10
A Christian's Ambition

Matthew 6:19-34

Everyone is ambitious to be or to do something. Childhood ambitions tend to follow certain stereotypes—to be an athlete, astronaut or movie star. Adults have their own narrow stereotypes too—to be wealthy, famous or powerful. But what should our Christian ambition be? In this passage Jesus helps us to choose well. He points out the folly of the wrong way and the wisdom of the right. Then he invites us to compare them and decide for ourselves.

1. When you were a child, what did you want to be when you grew up? Explain why.

2. Read Matthew 6:19-34. Why should we store up heavenly treasures rather than earthly ones (vv. 19-21)?

Does this mean that we cannot have personal property, savings accounts or insurance policies? Explain.

3. Practically speaking, how can we store up treasure in heaven?

4. How are physical and spiritual sight (or blindness) similar (vv. 22-23)?

5. Many people hold two jobs and are able to satisfy two bosses. So why would Jesus say that it is impossible to serve two masters—God and Money (v. 24)?

6. How will the crucial choices we make in verses 19-24 affect our ability to live free from worry (v. 25)?

7. According to Jesus, why are we foolish to worry about our physical and material needs (vv. 25-30)?

8. How does worry also reveal a lack of faith (v. 30)?

9. If God promises to feed and clothe his children, then why are many of them ill-clad and undernourished (see Mt 25:41-45)?

10. Give examples of how people today "run after all these things" that Jesus mentions (v. 31).

11. Why and how are our ambitions to be different from those of non-Christians (vv. 32-34)?

12. How has this passage challenged you to re-examine your goals and ambitions?

11
A Christian's Relationships:
Within God's Family

Matthew 7:1-12

The Christian community is a family, God's family. We need a strong awareness, therefore, of God as our Father and of our fellow Christians as brothers and sisters through Christ. At the same time we can never forget our responsibility to those outside the family, whom we long to see brought in. In Matthew 7:1-12 Jesus introduces us to these basic relationships.

1. Why are family relationships special?

2. Read Matthew 7:1-12. *Our relationship with our brother:* Why does Jesus tell us not to judge others (vv. 1-2)?

How do these verses expand on Jesus' statement about the merciful (5:7)?

3. According to Jesus, why are we often unfit to be judges (vv. 3-4)?

4. Some have assumed that Jesus was forbidding *all* judgment, even in law courts. How would you respond to this suggestion?

5. What steps must we take to truly help a brother or sister (v. 5)?

6. *Our relationship with "dogs" and "pigs":* This is startling language from the lips of Jesus. What kinds of people do you think he refers to as "dogs" and "pigs" (v. 6)?

Why is it futile, even dangerous, to talk with such people about the gospel?

7. *Our relationship with our heavenly Father:* What encouragement does Jesus give those who *ask, seek* and *knock* (vv. 7-8)?

How can we be assured of these promises (vv. 9-11)?

8. *Our relationship with all people:* The Jewish Talmud stated: "What is hateful to you, do not do to anyone else." Likewise, Confucius told his followers: "Do not to others what you would not wish done to you." How does the golden rule (v. 12) go beyond these commands?

9. In what sense does this rule sum up the Law and the Prophets?

10. Think of a relationship that is presently strained or broken. How can this passage help to mend that relationship?

12
A Christian's Relationships:
To False Prophets

Matthew 7:13-20

The history of the Christian church has been a long and dreary story of controversy with false teachers. Their value, in the overruling providence of God, is that they have presented the church with a challenge to think out and define truth. But they have also caused much damage. Jesus' warning "Watch out for false prophets" (7:15) is addressed to us all. If the church had heeded his warning and applied the tests in this passage, it would not be in the perilous state of theological and moral confusion in which it finds itself today.

1. Why are people likely to follow popular leaders or celebrities?

2. Read Matthew 7:13-20. How are the two gates different (vv. 13-14)?

3. In what sense is the gate of Christianity small and the road narrow?

4. Why do you think many people dislike the notion that there is only one true gate, road and destination?

5. Why is it significant that Jesus' warning about false prophets (vv. 15-20) comes immediately after his discussion of the narrow and wide gates?

6. Jesus says that false prophets "come to you *in sheep's clothing*" (v. 15)? What disguises might they wear today (see vv. 21-23)?

7. In what sense are these false prophets like ferocious wolves?

8. Jesus also says, "By their fruit you will recognize them" (v. 16). What kind of fruit does he have in mind?

How can the quality of the fruit reveal the quality of the tree?

9. How can we keep from becoming "witch hunters" as we seek to recognize false prophets?

10. *"Every* tree that does not bear good fruit is cut down and thrown into the fire" (v. 19). How can this warning to false prophets also keep us from becoming complacent as Christians?

13
A Christian's Commitment
Matthew 7:21-29

The Sermon on the Mount ends on the same note of radical choice we have been aware of throughout. Repeatedly Jesus has called his people to be different from everybody else. Our righteousness is to be deeper because it reaches even our hearts. Our love is to be broader because it embraces even our enemies. We have been confronted with two treasures, two masters, two ambitions, two gates and two roads. Now the moment of decision has come. Will we follow the crowd or follow our Father in heaven? Will we be swayed by the winds of public opinion or be ruled by God's Word, the revelation of his character and will? In this final passage, as throughout the Sermon, Jesus' overriding purpose is to present us with the inescapable necessity of choice.

1. We usually think of Bible reading as beneficial. How might reading the Bible also be dangerous?

2. Read Matthew 7:21-29. On the surface, what might we admire about those described in verses 21-23?

3. In spite of their admirable statements or actions, why does Jesus condemn such people?

4. How were the two houses similar and different (vv. 24-27)?

5. Why is it often difficult to tell the difference between genuine Christians and counterfeit ones?

6. How did the storms reveal what was previously unseen?

7. What kinds of storms might we face as Christians?

Why do they often reveal the quality of our lives?

8. The crowds were amazed at Jesus teaching, because he taught as one who had authority (vv. 28-29). In what ways was Jesus' authority demonstrated in his Sermon?

9. Why should Jesus' authority motivate us to obey him?

10. How do verses 21-29 provide a fitting conclusion to the Sermon on the Mount?

11. What are some of the "words" of Jesus you have heard in the Sermon on the Mount (v. 24)?

12. Think of one teaching from the Sermon that has challenged you most. How can you begin putting it into practice?

13. Ask the Lord to help you submit to his authority, especially in those areas where you feel disobedient or hypocritical.

Leader's Notes

Leading a Bible discussion can be an enjoyable and rewarding experience. But it can also be *scary*—especially if you've never done it before. If this is your feeling, you're in good company. When God asked Moses to lead the Israelites out of Egypt, he replied, "O Lord, please send someone else to do it!" (Ex 4:13).

When Solomon became king of Israel, he felt the task was far beyond his abilities. "I am only a little child and do not know how to carry out my duties. . . . Who is able to govern this great people of yours?" (1 Kings 3:7, 9).

When God called Jeremiah to be a prophet, he replied, "Ah, Sovereign LORD, . . . I do not know how to speak; I am only a child" (Jer 1:6).

The list goes on. The apostles were "unschooled, ordinary men" (Acts 4:13). Timothy was young, frail and frightened. Paul's "thorn in the flesh" made him feel weak. But God's response to all of his servants—including you—is essentially the same: "My grace is sufficient for you" (2 Cor 12:9). Relax. God helped these people in spite of their weaknesses, and he can help you in spite of your feelings of inadequacy.

There is another reason why you should feel encouraged. Leading a Bible discussion is not difficult if you follow certain guidelines. You don't need to be an expert on the Bible or a trained teacher. The suggestions listed below should enable you to effectively and enjoyably fulfill your role as leader.

Preparing to Lead

1. Ask God to help you understand and apply the passage to your own life. Unless this happens, you will not be prepared to lead others. Pray too for the various members of the group. Ask God to give you an enjoyable and profitable time together studying his Word.

2. As you begin each study, read and reread the assigned Bible passage to familiarize yourself with what the author is saying. In the case of book studies, you may want to read through the entire book prior to the first study. This will give you a helpful overview of its contents.

3. This study guide is based on the New International Version of the Bible. It will help you and the group if you use this translation as the basis for your study and discussion. Encourage others to use the NIV also, but allow them the freedom to use whatever translation they prefer.

4. Carefully work through each question in the study. Spend time in meditation and reflection as you formulate your answers.

5. Write your answers in the space provided in the study guide. This will help you to express your understanding of the passage clearly.

6. It might help you to have a Bible dictionary handy. Use it to look up any unfamiliar words, names or places. (For additional help on how to study a passage, see chapter five of *Leading Bible Discussions,* SU.)

7. Once you have finished your own study of the passage, familiarize yourself with the leader's notes for the study you are leading. These are designed to help you in several ways. First, they tell you the purpose the study guide author had in mind while writing the study. Take time to think through how the study questions work together to accomplish that purpose. Second, the notes provide you with additional background information or comments on some of the questions. This information can be useful if people have difficulty understanding or answering a question. Third, the leader's notes can alert you to potential problems you may encounter during the study.

8. If you wish to remind yourself of anything mentioned in the leader's notes, make a note to yourself below that question in the study.

Leading the Study

1. Begin the study on time. Unless you are leading an evangelistic Bible study, open with prayer, asking God to help you to understand and apply the passage.

2. Be sure that everyone in your group has a study guide. Encourage them to prepare beforehand for each discussion by working through the questions in the guide.

3. At the beginning of your first time together, explain that these studies are meant to be discussions not lectures. Encourage the members of the group to participate. However, do not put pressure on those who may be hesitant to speak during the first few sessions.

4. Read the introductory paragraph at the beginning of the discussion. This will orient the group to the passage being studied.

5. Read the passage aloud if you are studying one chapter or less. You may choose to do this yourself, or someone else may read if he or she has been asked to do so prior to the study. Longer passages may occasionally be read in parts at different times during the study. Some studies may cover several chapters. In such cases reading aloud would probably take too much time, so the group members should simply read the assigned passages prior to the study.

6. As you begin to ask the questions in the guide, keep several things in mind. First, the questions are designed to be used just as they are written. If you wish, you may simply read them aloud to the group. Or you may prefer to express them in your own words. However, unnecessary rewording of the questions is not recommended.

Second, the questions are intended to guide the group toward understanding and applying the *main idea* of the passage. The author of the guide has stated his or her view of this central idea in the *purpose* of the study in the leader's notes. You should try to understand how the passage expresses this idea and how the study questions work together to lead the group in that direction.

There may be times when it is appropriate to deviate from the study guide. For example, a question may have already been answered. If so, move on to the next question. Or someone may raise an important question not covered in the guide. Take time to discuss it! The important thing is to use discretion. There may be many routes you can travel to reach the goal of the study. But the easiest route is usually the one the author has suggested.

7. Avoid answering your own questions. If necessary, repeat or rephrase them until they are clearly understood. An eager group quickly becomes passive and silent if they think the leader will do most of the talking.

8. Don't be afraid of silence. People may need time to think about the question before formulating their answers.

9. Don't be content with just one answer. Ask, "What do the rest of you think?" or "Anything else?" until several people have given answers to the question.

10. Acknowledge all contributions. Try to be affirming whenever possible. Never reject an answer. If it is clearly wrong, ask, "Which verse led you to that conclusion?" or again, "What do the rest of you think?"

11. Don't expect every answer to be addressed to you, even though this will probably happen at first. As group members become more at ease, they will begin to truly interact with each other. This is one sign of a healthy discussion.

12. Don't be afraid of controversy. It can be very stimulating. If you don't resolve an issue completely, don't be frustrated. Move on and keep it in mind for later. A subsequent study may solve the problem.

13. Stick to the passage under consideration. It should be the source for answering the questions. Discourage the group from unnecessary cross-referencing. Likewise, stick to the subject and avoid going off on tangents.

14. Periodically summarize what the *group* has said about the passage. This helps to draw together the various ideas mentioned and gives continuity to the study. But don't preach.

15. Conclude your time together with conversational prayer. Be sure to ask God's help to apply those things which you learned in the study.

16. End on time.

Many more suggestions and helps are found in *Leading Bible Discussions* (IVP). Reading and studying through that would be well worth your time.

Components of Small Groups

A healthy small group should do more than study the Bible. There are four components you should consider as you structure your time together.

Nurture. Being a part of a small group should be a nurturing and edifying experience. You should grow in your knowledge and love of God and each other. If we are to properly love God, we must know and keep his commandments (Jn 14:15). That is why Bible study should be a foundational part of your small group. But you can be nurtured by other things as well. You can memorize Scripture, read and discuss a book, or occasionally listen to a tape of a good speaker.

Community. Most people have a need for close friendships. Your small group can be an excellent place to cultivate such relationships. Allow time for informal interaction before and after the study. Have a time of sharing during the meeting. Do fun things together as a group, such as a potluck supper or a picnic. Have someone bring refreshments to the meeting. Be creative!

Worship. A portion of your time together can be spent in worship and prayer. Praise God together for who he is. Thank him for what he has done and is doing in your lives and in the world. Pray for each other's needs. Ask God to help you to apply what you have learned. Sing hymns together.

Mission. Many small groups decide to work together in some form of outreach. This can be a practical way of applying what you have learned. You can host a series of evangelistic discussions for your friends or neighbors. You can visit people at a home for the elderly. Help a widow with cleaning or repair jobs around her home. Such projects can have a transforming influence on your group.

For a detailed discussion of the nature and function of small groups, read *Small Group Leaders' Handbook* (Downers Grove, Ill: InterVarsity Press) or *Good Things Come in Small Groups* (Scripture Union).

Study 1. A Christian's Character (Part 1). Matthew 5:1-12.
Purpose: To consider the Christian's character in relation to God.
Question 1. Every study begins with an "approach" question, which is meant to be asked before the passage is read. These questions are important for several reasons.

First, they help the group to warm up to each other. No matter how well a group may know each other, there is always a stiffness that needs to be overcome before people will begin to talk openly. A good question will break the ice.

Second, approach questions get people thinking along the lines of the topic of the study. Most people will have lots of different things going on in their minds (dinner, an important meeting coming up, how to get the car fixed) that will have nothing to do with the study. A creative question will get their attention and draw them into the discussion.

Third, approach questions can reveal where our thoughts or feelings need to be transformed by Scripture. This is why it is especially important not to read the passage before the approach question is asked. The passage will tend to color the honest reactions people would otherwise give because they are of course supposed to think the way the Bible does. Giving honest responses to various issues before they find out what the Bible says may help them to see where their thoughts or attitudes need to be changed.

Question 2. This LifeGuide Bible Study draws on material first published in *The Message of the Sermon on the Mount,* a volume I have written in The Bible Speaks Today series (IVP). I recommend that book as supplementary reading, especially for the person leading the study.

The Greek word *makarios* can and does mean "happy." So J. B. Phillips translates the opening words of each beatitude, "How happy are. . . !" And several commentators have explained them as Jesus' prescription for human happiness. Nevertheless, it is seriously misleading to render *makarios* "happy." For happiness is a subjective state, whereas Jesus is making an objective judgment about these people. He is declaring not what they may feel like ("happy"), but what God thinks of them and what on that account they are—("blessed").

Question 3. The poverty and hunger to which Jesus refers in the beatitudes are spiritual states. It is true that the Aramaic word Jesus used may have been simply "poor," as in Luke's version. But then "the poor," God's poor, were already a clearly defined group in the Old Testament, and Matthew will have been correct to translate "poor in spirit." For "the poor" were not so much the poverty stricken as the pious who—partly because they were needy, downtrodden, oppressed or in other ways afflicted—had put their faith and hope in God.

Question 4. One might almost translate this second beatitude "Happy are the unhappy" in order to draw attention to the startling paradox it contains. It is plain from the context that those here promised comfort are not primarily those who mourn the loss of a loved one, but those who mourn the loss of their innocence, their righteousness, their self-respect. It is not the sorrow of bereavement to which Christ refers, but the sorrow of repentance.

Question 6. Such mourners, who bewail their own sinfulness, will be comforted by the only comfort which can relieve their distress, namely the free forgiveness of God. According to the Old Testament, Messiah was to be "the Comforter" who would "bind up the brokenhearted"

(Is 61:1-3). And Christ does pour oil into our wounds and speak peace
to our sore, scarred consciences. Yet we still mourn over the havoc of
suffering and death which sin spreads throughout the world. For only
in the final state of glory will Christ's comfort be complete; for only
then will sin be no more, and "God will wipe away every tear from
their eyes" (Rev 7:17).

Question 7. We tend to think of "the meek" as weak and effeminate.
Yet the Greek adjective means "gentle," "humble," "considerate" and
"courteous." Dr. Lloyd-Jones sums it up admirably: "Meekness is essentially a true view of oneself, expressing itself in attitude and conduct with respect to others. . . . The man who is truly meek is the one
who is truly amazed that God and man can think of him as well as they
do and treat him as well as they do" (*Studies in the Sermon on the
Mount* [Leicester, England: Inter-Varsity Press, 1977], pp. 68-69).

Question 10. Legal righteousness is justification, a right relationship
with God. Moral righteousness is that righteousness of character and
conduct which pleases God. Social righteousness, as we learn from the
Law and the Prophets, is concerned with seeking humanity's liberation
from oppression, together with the promotion of civil rights, justice in
the law courts, integrity in business dealings, and honor in home and
family affairs.

Study 2. A Christian's Character (Part 2). Matthew 5:1-12.
Purpose: To consider a Christian's character in his or her relations and
duties to other people.

Question 2. Richard Lenski in *The Interpretation of St. Matthew's
Gospel* (Augsburg, 1964) helpfully distinguishes mercy from grace:
"The noun *eleos* (mercy) . . . always deals with what we see of pain,
misery and distress, these results of sin; and *charis* (grace) always deals
with the sin and guilt itself. The one extends relief, the other pardon;
the one cures, heals, helps, the other cleanses and reinstates" (p. 191).

Question 5. The idea that "pure in heart" refers to inward purity is
certainly consistent with the whole Sermon on the Mount, which requires heart-righteousness rather than mere rule-righteousness. Never-

theless, in the context of the other beatitudes, "pure in heart" seems
to refer in some sense to our relationships. Thus the pure in heart, in
their relations with both God and others, are free from falsehood. Their
very heart—including their thoughts and motives—is pure, unmixed
with anything devious, ulterior or base. Hypocrisy and deceit are ab-
horrent to them; they are without guile.

Question 6. Only the pure in heart will see God, see him now with
the eye of faith and see his glory in the hereafter, for only the utterly
sincere can bear the dazzling vision in whose light the darkness of
deceit must vanish and by whose fire all shams are burned up.

Question 9. A person who avoids conflict is not necessarily a peacemaker. Facing issues and helping people work through them is part
of peacemaking.

Questions 10-11. It may seem strange that Jesus should pass from
peacemaking to persecution, from the work of reconciliation to the
experience of hostility. Yet however hard we may try to make peace
with some people, they refuse to live at peace with us. Not all attempts
at reconciliation succeed. Indeed, some take the initiative to oppose
us, and in particular to "revile" or slander us. This is not because of
our foibles or idiosyncrasies, but "because of righteousness" (v. 10)
and "because of me" (v. 11), that is, because they find distasteful the
righteousness for which we hunger and thirst (v. 6), and because they
have rejected the Christ we seek to follow. Persecution is simply the
clash between two irreconcilable value systems.

Study 3. A Christian's Influence. Matthew 5:13-16.
Purpose: To consider the kind of influence Jesus expects us to have
on those around us.

Question 1. The establishment of hospitals all over the world, the
abolition of slavery, the feeding of the hungry and the call for peace
in times of conflict are just a few of the actions Christians have taken
to preserve society.

Question 2. Be sure to notice that questions 2-5 look at our role as
salt, while questions 6-10 look at our role as *light.* Then questions 11-

12 draw the two together.

Question 5. Strictly speaking, salt can never lose its saltiness. But Dr. David Turk has suggested to me that what was then popularly called "salt" was in fact a white powder (perhaps from around the Dead Sea) which, while containing sodium chloride, also contained much else, since in those days there were no refineries. Of this dust the sodium chloride was probably the most soluble component and so the most easily washed out. The residue of white powder still looked like salt, and was doubtless still called salt, but it neither tasted nor acted like salt. It was just road dust.

Question 6. The effects of salt and light are complementary. The function of salt is largely negative: it prevents decay. The function of light is positive: it illumines the darkness. For it is one thing to stop the spread of evil; it is another to promote the spread of truth, beauty and goodness. Jesus calls us to do both.

Question 8. True, some non-Christians adopt a deceptive veneer of Christian culture. Some professing Christians, on the other hand, seem indistinguishable from non-Christians and so deny their Christian name by their non-Christian behavior. Yet the essential difference remains. Jesus said they are as different as light from darkness, as different as salt from decay and disease. We serve neither God nor ourselves nor the world by attempting to obliterate or even minimize this difference. Probably the greatest tragedy of the church throughout its long and checkered history has been its constant tendency to conform to the prevailing culture instead of developing a Christian counterculture.

Question 9. Jesus says we give light by our "good deeds." It seems that "good deeds" is a general expression to cover everything Christians say and do because they are Christians, every outward and visible manifestation of their Christian faith. They express not only our loyalty to God, but our care for others as well. Indeed, the primary meaning of "deeds" must be practical, visible acts of compassion. It is when people see these, Jesus said, that they will glorify God, for they embody the good news of his love which we proclaim. Without them our gospel loses its credibility and our God his honor.

Question 10. A Christian's character as described in the beatitudes and a Christian's influence as defined in the salt and light metaphors are related to one another. Our *influence* depends on our *character*.

Study 4. A Christian's Righteousness: Christ, the Christian & the Law. Matthew 5:17-20.
Purpose: To understand the meaning of Christian righteousness and the place of Scripture in our lives.
Question 2. If the group has some trouble with this question, you might ask them to look at the pronouns to see if this sheds any light on the different emphasis of each part. Verses 17-18 discuss Christ and the law, while 19-20 consider the Christian and the law.
Question 3. Jesus spoke with his own authority. He loved to use a formula no ancient prophet or modern scribe had ever used, "Truly I say to you," speaking in his own name and with his own authority. What was this authority of his? Was he setting himself up as an authority against the sacred law, the Word of God? So it seemed to some. Hence their question, spoken or unspoken, which Jesus now answered unequivocally: "Do not think that I have come to abolish the Law or the Prophets."
Question 4. The verb translated "to fulfill" *(plerosai)* means literally "to fill" and indicates, as Chrysostom expressed it, that "his [Christ's] sayings were no repeal of the former, but a drawing out and filling up of them."

Christ fulfilled the doctrinal teaching of the Old Testament by bringing its partial revelation to completion by his person, his teaching and his work. He fulfilled predictive prophecy because what was predicted about the Messiah came to pass in him. And he fulfilled the ethical precepts of the Old Testament by obeying them and giving us their true interpretation. The group might also discuss how Jesus fulfilled the ceremonial laws, including the priesthood and sacrifices.
Question 5. The "smallest letter" of the Hebrew alphabet was a *yod,* almost as small as a comma. The "least stroke of a pen" probably refers to one of the tiny hooks or projections which distinguished some

Hebrew letters from others. Jesus' reference now was only to "the Law" rather than to "the Law and the Prophets" as in the previous verse, but we have no reason to suppose that he was deliberately omitting the Prophets; "the Law" was a comprehensive term for the total divine revelation of the Old Testament. None of it will pass away or be discarded, he says, not a single letter or part of a letter, until it has all been fulfilled. And this fulfillment will not be complete until the heaven and the earth themselves pass away.

Question 7. Our Lord's statement in verse 20 must certainly have astonished his first hearers as it astonishes us today. But Christian righteousness far surpasses pharisaic righteousness in kind rather than in degree. It is not so much that Christians succeed in keeping 240 commandments when the best Pharisees may only have scored 230. No, Christian righteousness is greater than pharisaic righteousness because it is deeper, being a righteousness of the heart.

The scribes and Pharisees were actually attempting (according to Jesus) to make Old Testament commands more manageable and less exacting by describing in tortuous detail what it actually meant to obey particular laws. Jesus sought to reverse this. As we will see in the six "You have heard it said" passages (see vv. 21, 27, 31, 33, 38 and 43) to be discussed in the next three studies, Jesus is preaching a much more demanding interpretation of Scripture than even the Pharisees. Because this may not become clear to the group during this study, you may want to ask them to hold their questions until you have had a chance to finish studying Matthew 5.

Question 9. The apostle Paul summarizes the "law of love" in Galatians 5:14, "The entire law is summed up in a single command: 'Love your neighbor as yourself.' " However, some people mistakenly assume that if our actions are motivated by love, then we can do whatever we wish—even those things that are contrary toward the law.

In every generation of the Christian era there have been those who could not accommodate themselves to Christ's attitude toward the law. The famous second-century heretic Marcion, who rewrote the New Testament by eliminating its references to the Old, naturally erased this passage. Some of his followers went even further. They dared even to reverse its meaning by exchanging the verbs so that the sentence read: "I have come not to fulfill the law and the prophets, but to abolish them"!

Their counterparts today seem to be those who have embraced the so-called new morality. They regard the law as rigid and authoritarian, and (just like the Pharisees) they attempt to "relax" its authority, to loosen its hold. So they declare the category of law abolished (which Jesus said he had not come to abolish) and they set law and love at variance with each other (in a way in which Jesus never did). No, Jesus disagreed with the Pharisees' *interpretation* of the law; he never disagreed with their acceptance of its *authority*. Rather the reverse. In the strongest possible terms he asserted its authority as God's written Word, and called his disciples to accept its true and deeply exacting interpretation.

Study 5. A Christian's Righteousness: Avoiding Anger & Lust. Matthew 5:21-30.

Purpose: To understand how anger and lust are related to the commandments against murder and adultery.

Question 2. Verse 21 is not a prohibition against taking all human life in any and every circumstance. This is clear from the fact that the same Mosaic law, which forbids killing in the Decalogue, elsewhere calls for it both in the form of capital punishment and in the wars designed to exterminate the corrupt pagan tribes which inhabited the Promised Land.

Question 3. The scribes and Pharisees were evidently seeking to restrict the application of the sixth commandment to the deed of murder alone, to the act of spilling human blood in homicide. If they refrained from this, they considered that they had kept the commandment. And this apparently is what the rabbis taught the people. But Jesus disagreed with them. The true application of the prohibition was much wider, he maintained. It included thoughts and words as well as deeds, anger and insult as well as murder.

Not all anger is evil, as is evident from the wrath of God, which is always holy and pure. And even fallen human beings may sometimes feel righteous anger, although, being fallen, we should ensure that even this is slow to rise and quick to die down (Jas 1:19 and Eph 4:26-27). The reference of Jesus, then, is to unrighteous anger, the anger of pride, vanity, hatred, malice and revenge.

Question 5. In these verses Jesus proceeds to give a practical application of the principles he has just enunciated. His theme is that if anger and insult are so serious and so dangerous, then we must avoid them at all cost and take action as speedily as possible. We must never allow an estrangement to remain, still less to grow. We must not delay to put it right. If we want to avoid committing murder in God's sight, we must take every possible positive step to live in peace and love with all people.

Question 6. There is not the slightest suggestion here that natural sexual relations within the commitment of marriage are anything but God-given and beautiful. We may thank God that the Song of Solomon is contained in the canon of Scripture, for there is not Victorian prudery there but rather the uninhibited delight of lovers, of bride and bridegroom in each other. No, the teaching of Jesus here refers to unlawful sex outside marriage, whether practiced by married or unmarried people.

Similarly, Jesus' allusion is to all forms of immorality. To argue that the reference is only to a man lusting after a woman and not vice versa, or only to a married man and not an unmarried, since the offender is said to commit "adultery" not "fornication," is to be guilty of the very casuistry which Jesus was condemning in the Pharisees. His emphasis is that any and every sexual practice which is immoral in deed is immoral also in look and thought.

Question 7. On the surface it is a startling command to pluck out an offending eye, to cut off an offending hand or foot. A few Christians, whose zeal greatly exceeded their wisdom, have taken Jesus literally. The best known example is the third-century scholar, Origen of Alexandria, who actually made himself a eunuch. Not long after, in A.D.

325, the Council of Nicea was right to forbid this barbarous practice.

The command to get rid of troublesome eyes, hands and feet is an example of our Lord's use of dramatic figures of speech. What he was advocating was not a literal physical self-maiming, but a ruthless moral self-denial. Not mutilation but mortification is the path of holiness he taught, and mortification or "taking up the cross" to follow Christ means to reject sinful practices so resolutely that we die to them or put them to death (see Mk 8:34; Rom 8:13; Gal 5:24; Col 3:5).

Question 10. This question might be too threatening in some groups. If this is true of your group, you might suggest that people reflect on the question silently.

Study 6. A Christian's Righteousness: In Marriage & Speech. Matthew 5:31-37; 19:3-9.

Purpose: To consider why we should be faithful in marriage and honest in speech.

Question 2. The debate between Rabbi Shammai and Rabbi Hillel centered on the interpretation of Deuteronomy 24:1-4, especially the phrase "he finds *something indecent* about her" (v. 1). Rabbi Shammai took a rigorist line and taught that *something indecent* referred to some grave matrimonial offense. Rabbi Hillel, on the other hand, interpreted this phrase in the widest possible way to include a wife's most trivial offenses. If she proved to be an incompetent cook and burnt her husband's food, or if he lost interest in her because of her plain looks and because he became enamored with some other more beautiful woman, these things were "something indecent" and justified him in divorcing her. The Pharisees seem to have been attracted by Rabbi Hillel's laxity, which explains the form of their question: "Is it lawful for a man to divorce his wife *for any and every reason?*" In other words, they wanted to know whose side Jesus was on in the contemporary debate, and whether he belonged to the school of rigorism or of laxity.

Questions 3-4. The Pharisees were preoccupied with the grounds for divorce; Jesus with the institution of marriage. Notice that Jesus' reply was not a reply. He declined to answer their question. Instead, he asked a counterquestion about their reading of Scripture. He referred them back to Genesis, both to the creation of humanity as male and female (Gen 1) and to the institution of marriage (Gen 2) by which a man leaves his parents and cleaves to his wife and the two become one. This biblical definition implies that marriage is both exclusive ("a man . . . his wife") and permanent ("be united" to his wife). It is these two aspects of marriage which Jesus selects for emphasis in his comments which follow.

Question 5. The Pharisees emphasized the giving of a divorce certificate, as if this were the most important part of the Mosaic provision, and then referred to both the certificate and the divorce as "commands" of Moses. But a careful reading of Deuteronomy 24:1-4 reveals something quite different. To begin with, the whole paragraph hinges on a long series of conditional clauses. This may be brought out in the following paraphrase: "After a man has married a wife, *if* he finds something indecent in her, and *if* he gives her a certificate of divorce and divorces her and she leaves, and *if* she marries again, and *if* her second husband gives her a certificate of divorce and divorces her, or *if* her second husband dies, *then* her first husband who divorced her is forbidden to remarry her." The thrust of the passage is to prohibit remarriage to one's own divorced partner. The reason for this regulation is obscure. For our purposes here it is enough to observe that this prohibition is the only command in the whole passage; there is certainly no command to a husband to divorce his wife, nor even any encouragement to do so. All there is, instead, is a reference to certain necessary procedures *if* a divorce takes place; and therefore at the very most a reluctant permission is implied and a current practice is tolerated. Yet even the divine concession was in principle inconsistent with the divine institution of marriage, as Jesus points out in 19:8.

If you are able to control discussion enough so that too much time is not taken up here, you might want to have the group turn to Deuteronomy 24:1-4. But if your group is talkative, you might just want to summarize what is mentioned above if it would be helpful in your discussion.

An unwillingness or inability to forgive a marriage partner and be reconciled might reveal how hardened we are by sin to the grace and mercy of God.

Question 6. Jesus allows only one exception to the rule that remarriage after divorce results in adultery. That is the so-called exception clause in 5:32 and 19:9: "except for marital unfaithfulness." Conservative scholars disagree about why it is omitted from the parallel passages in Mark and Luke. They also disagree about the meaning of "marital unfaithfulness" *(porneia)*.

It seems likely that its absence from Mark and Luke is due not to their ignorance of it but to their acceptance of it as something taken for granted. After all, under the Mosaic law adultery was punishable by death (although the death penalty for this offense seems to have generally fallen into disuse by the time of Jesus), so nobody would have questioned that marital unfaithfulness was a just ground for divorce. Even the rival Rabbis Shammai and Hillel were agreed about this.

The Greek word for "marital unfaithfulness" is normally translated "fornication," denoting the immorality of the unmarried, and is often distinguished from adultery, the immorality of the married. For this reason some have argued that the exception clause permits divorce if some premarital sexual sin is later discovered. But the Greek word is not precise enough to be limited in this way. It is derived from *porne,* "prostitute," without specifying whether she (or her client) is married or unmarried. Further, it is used in the Septuagint for the unfaithfulness of Israel, Yahweh's bride, as exemplified in Hosea's wife, Gomer. It seems, therefore, that we must agree with R. V. G. Tasker's conclusion that *porneia* is "a comprehensive word, including adultery, fornication and unnatural vice" (*The Gospel according to St. Matthew,* Tyndale New Testament Commentaries [Grand Rapids, Mich.: Eerdmans, 1961], p. 184).

Question 9. Verse 33 is not an accurate quotation of any one law of Moses. At the same time, it is an accurate summary of several Old Testament precepts which require people who make vows to keep them. These include Exodus 20:7, Leviticus 19:12, Numbers 30:2 and Deuteronomy 23:21. The Pharisees got to work on these awkward prohibitions and tried to restrict them. They shifted people's attention away from the vow itself and the need to keep it to the formula used in making it. Jesus teaches that a vow is binding irrespective of its accompanying formula. That being so, the real implication of the law is that we must keep our promises and be people of our word. Then vows become unnecessary.

Question 10. The Anabaptists took this line in the sixteenth century and most Quakers still do today. While admiring their desire not to compromise, one can still perhaps question whether their interpretation is not excessively literalistic. Jesus emphasized in his teaching that honest people do not need to resort to oaths; he did not say they should refuse to take an oath if required by some external authority to do so.

Question 11. Question 9 concerns the negative effects of oaths. This question covers why oaths aren't needed (even if there were no harmful aspects to them). As Christians, our simple answers should carry all the weight needed to convince people that we are honest and reliable, that we will follow through on what we promise. People should be able to trust us because of our character rooted in Christ.

Study 7. A Christian's Righteousness: Loving Our Enemies. Matthew 5:38-48.

Purpose: To learn how and why we should love our enemies.

Question 2. This principle was also stated in Leviticus 24:20 and Deuteronomy 19:21. The context makes it clear beyond question that this was an instruction to the judges of Israel. Indeed, they are mentioned in Deuteronomy 19:17-18. It expressed the principle of an exact retribution, whose purpose was both to lay the foundation of justice, specifying the punishment which a wrongdoer deserved, and to limit the compensation of his victim to an exact equivalent and no more.

It is almost certain that by the time of Jesus literal retaliation for damages had been replaced in Jewish legal practice by money penalties or "damages." Indeed, there is evidence of this much earlier. Exodus 21:26-27 states that if a man strikes his slave so as to destroy his eye or knock out his tooth, instead of losing his own eye or tooth (which he would deserve but which would be no compensation to the disabled slave), he must lose his slave: "He must let the servant go free to compensate for the eye [or tooth]." We may be quite sure that in other cases too this penalty was not physically exacted, except in the case of murder ("life for life"); it was commuted to a payment of damages.

Question 3. The scribes and Pharisees tried to use this principle to justify personal revenge, although the law explicitly forbade this: "Do not seek revenge or bear a grudge against one of your people, but love your neighbor as yourself" (Lev 19:18). Thus, "this excellent, if stern, principle of judicial retribution was being utilized as an excuse for the very thing it was instituted to abolish, namely personal revenge" (John W. Wenham, *Christ and the Bible* [Leicester: Inter-Varsity Press, 1972], p. 35).

Questions 7-10. We cannot take Jesus' command, "Do not resist an evil person," as an absolute prohibition of the use of all force (including the police) unless we are prepared to say that the Bible contradicts itself and the apostles misunderstood Jesus. For the New Testament teaches that the state is a divine institution, commissioned (through its executive officebearers) both to punish the wrongdoer; that is, to resist one who is evil to the point of making him bear the penalty of his evil and to reward those who do good (Rom 13).

Likewise, Christ does not intend for his followers to be doormats. His illustrations and personal example depict not the weakling who offers no resistance. He himself challenged the high priest when questioned by him in court (Jn 18:19-23). And the apostle Paul once "resisted" (same Greek word) the apostle Peter to his face (Gal 2:11-14). They depict rather the strong man whose control of himself and love for others are so powerful that he rejects absolutely every conceivable form of retaliation. The only limit to the Christian's generosity will be a limit which love itself might impose.

So the command of Jesus not to resist evil should not properly be used to justify either temperamental weakness, political anarchy or even total pacifism. Instead, what Jesus here demands of all his followers is a personal attitude to evildoers which is prompted by mercy not justice, which renounces retaliation so completely as to risk further costly suffering, which is never governed by the desire to cause them harm but always by the determination to serve their highest good.

Question 11. It had been written of Jesus in the Old Testament: "I offered my back to those who beat me, my cheeks to those who pulled out my beard; I did not hide my face from mocking and spitting" (Is 50:6). And in the actual event the Jewish police spat on him, blindfolded him and struck him in the face, and then the Roman soldiers followed suit. They crowned him with thorns, clothed him in the imperial purple, invested him with a scepter of reed, jeered at him, "Hail, King of the Jews," knelt before him in mock homage, spat in his face and struck him with their hands (Mk 14:65; 15:16-20). And Jesus, with the infinite dignity of self-control and love, held his peace. He demonstrated his total refusal to retaliate by allowing them to continue their cruel mockery until they had finished.

Question 12. The Christian's righteousness, whether expressed in purity, honesty or charity, will show to whom we belong. Our Christian calling is to imitate not the world but the Father. And it is by this imitation of him that the Christian counterculture becomes visible.

Some holiness teachers have built upon verse 48 great dreams of the possibility of reaching in this life a state of sinless perfection. But the words of Jesus cannot be pressed into meaning this without causing discord in the Sermon. For he has already indicated in the beatitudes that a hunger and thirst after righteousness is a perpetual characteristic of his disciples, and in the next chapter he will teach us to pray constantly, "Forgive us our debts" (6:12). Both the hunger for righteousness and the prayer for forgiveness, being continuous, are clear indications that Jesus did not expect his followers to become morally perfect in this life. The context shows that the "perfection" he means relates to love, the perfect love of God which is shown even to those who do not return it. We are to love our enemies with the merciful, inclusive love of God.

Study 8. A Christian's Religion. Matthew 6:1-6, 16-18.
Purpose: To consider proper and improper motives for our religious conduct.
Question 2. Verses 7-15 will be covered in the next study.

The discrepancy is only verbal, not substantial. The clue lies in the fact that Jesus is speaking against different sins. It is our human cowardice which made him say, "Let your light shine before men," and our human vanity which made him tell us to beware of practicing our piety before men. A. B. Bruce sums it up well when he writes that we are to "show when tempted to *hide*" and "hide when tempted to *show*" (*Commentary on the Synoptic Gospels,* The Expositor's Greek Testament, ed. W. Robertson Nicholl [London: Hodder, 1897], p. 116). Our good works must be public so that our light shines; our religious devotions must be secret lest we boast about them.
Question 3. The three illustrations follow an identical pattern. In vivid and deliberately humorous imagery Jesus paints a picture of the hypocrite's way of being religious. It is the way of ostentation. Such receive the reward they want, the applause of others. With this he contrasts the Christian way, which is secret, and the only reward which Christians want, the blessing of God who is their heavenly Father and who sees in secret. Taking time to picture the scenes Jesus is painting will help bring home the vividness of his comments to his original hearers—and to us as well.
Question 4. The question is not so much what the hand is doing (giving over some cash or writing a check) but what the heart is thinking while the hand is doing it.
Question 6. There was nothing wrong in standing to pray, for this was the usual posture for prayer among the Jews. Nor were they necessarily mistaken to pray *on the street corners* as well as *in the synagogues* if their motive was to break down segregated religion and bring their

recognition of God out of the holy places into the secular life of every day. But Jesus uncovered their true motive as they stood in synagogue or street with hands uplifted to heaven in order that they might *be seen by men.* Behind their piety lurked their pride. What they really wanted was applause. They got it. "They have received their reward in full." Rather than becoming absorbed in the mechanics of secrecy, we need to remember that the purpose of Jesus' emphasis on "secret" prayer is to purify our motives in praying.

Question 9. R. V. G. Tasker points out that the Greek word for the "room" into which we are to withdraw to pray *(tameion)* "was used for the storeroom where treasures might be kept." The implication may be, then, that "there are treasures already awaiting" us when we pray *(Matthew,* p. 73). Certainly the hidden rewards of prayer are too many to enumerate. In words of the apostle Paul, when we cry, "Abba, Father," the Holy Spirit witnesses with our spirit that we are indeed God's children, and we are granted a strong assurance of his father-hood and love (Rom 5:5; 8:16). He lifts the light of his face upon us and gives us his peace (Num 6:26). He refreshes our soul, satisfies our hunger, quenches our thirst. We know we are no longer orphans, for the Father has adopted us; no longer prodigals, for we have been forgiven; no longer alienated, for we have come home.

Question 10. Strictly speaking, fasting is a total abstention from food. It can be legitimately extended, however, to mean going without food partially or totally, for shorter or longer periods. There can be no doubt that in Scripture fasting has to do in various ways with self-denial and self-discipline. First and foremost, to "fast" and to "humble ourselves before God" are virtually equivalent terms (Ps 35:13; Is 58:3, 5). Some-times this was an expression of penitence for past sins. When people were deeply distressed over their sin and guilt, they would both weep and fast (Neh 9:1-2; Jon 3:5; Dan 9:2-19; 10:2-3; Acts 9:9). We are not to humble ourselves before God only in penitence for past sin, how-ever, but also in dependence on him for future mercy. For if penitence and fasting go together in Scripture, "prayer and fasting" are even more often coupled (Ex 24:18; 2 Chron 20:1-4; Esther 4:16; Ezra 8:21-23; Mt

4:1-2; Acts 13:1-3; 14:23).

Our fasting can also be a means of self-discipline. A voluntary ab-
stinence from food is one way of increasing our self-control (1 Cor
9:24-27). Likewise, fasting can be a deliberate doing without in order
to share what we might have eaten (or its cost) with the undernourished (Is 58:1-7).

Study 9. A Christian's Prayer. Matthew 6:7-15.
Purpose: To learn how we should pray.
Question 2. Jesus is not condemning perseverance in prayer but
rather verbosity, especially in those who speak without thinking.
Question 4. Believers do not pray to God to tell him things he doesn't
know or to motivate him to keep his promises or to urge him to do
what he really doesn't want to do at all. Rather, prayer is for our
benefit—to exercise our faith and to cast our worries on him. As Luther
put it in his commentary on this passage, "By our praying . . . we are
instructing ourselves more than we are him."
Question 5. In the first part of this question you are simply looking
for what verses are covered in each half of the Lord's Prayer: verses 9-
10 and 11-13. Then, in the second part of the question, look for the
main subject of each half. If the group needs help, tell them to notice
that in the second half of the Lord's Prayer the possessive adjective
changes from "your" to "our," as we turn from God's affairs to our own.

The well-known phrase "for yours is the kingdom and the power
and the glory forever" is not found in the earliest manuscripts.
Question 6. The words *in heaven* denote not the place of God's
abode so much as the authority and power at his command as the
creator and ruler of all things. Thus he combines fatherly love with
heavenly power, and what his love directs his power is able to perform.
Question 7. The name of God is not a combination of the letters *G,
O* and *D*. The name stands for the person who bears it, for his character
and activity. So God's "name" is God himself as he is in himself and
has revealed himself. His name is already holy in that it is separate from
and exalted over every other name. But we pray that it may be *hal-*

lowed, ("treated as holy"), because we ardently desire that due honor may be given to it, that is to him whose name it is, in our own lives, in the church and in the world.

Question 8. The kingdom of God is his royal rule. Again, as he is already holy so he is already King, reigning in absolute sovereignty over both nature and history. Yet when Jesus came he announced a new and special break-in of the kingly rule of God, with all the blessings of salvation and the demands of submission which the divine rule implies. To pray that his kingdom may "come" is to pray both that it may grow, as through the church's witness people submit to Jesus, and that soon it will be consummated when Jesus returns in glory to take his power and reign.

Question 9. You might ask the group to think of situations in which we could demonstrate greater concern for God's name than our name, God's kingdom than our "kingdom" and God's will than our will.

Question 10. Early church fathers like Tertullian, Cyprian and Augustine thought the reference was either to "the invisible bread of the Word of God" (Augustine) or to the Lord's Supper. Jerome, in the Vulgate, translated the Greek word for "daily" by the monstrous adjective "supersubstantial"; he also meant the Holy Communion. A more ordinary, down-to-earth interpretation seems most likely—just as the Lord daily provided manna for the Israelites in the desert (Ex 16:4).

Question 11. Jesus certainly does not mean that our forgiveness of others earns us the right to be forgiven. Rather he means that God forgives only the penitent and that one of the chief evidences of true penitence is a forgiving spirit. Once our eyes have been opened to see the enormity of our offense against God, the injuries which others have done to us appear by comparison extremely trifling. If, on the other hand, we have an exaggerated view of the offenses of others, it proves that we have minimized our own.

Question 12. It is probable that the prayer is more that we may overcome temptation, than that we may avoid it. Perhaps we could paraphrase the whole request as, "Do not allow us so to be led into temptation that overwhelms us, but rescue us from the evil one." So

behind these words that Jesus gave us to pray are the implications that
the devil is too strong for us, that we are too weak to stand up to him,
but that our heavenly Father will deliver us if we call on him.

Study 10. A Christian's Ambition. Matthew 6:19-34.
Purpose: To learn why we should not be ambitious for material security but rather for God's rule.
Question 2. What Jesus forbids his followers is the *selfish* accumulation of goods ("Do not store up *for yourselves* treasures on earth"):
extravagant and luxurious living; the hardheartedness which does not
feel the colossal need of the world's underprivileged people; the foolish fantasy that a person's life consists in the abundance of his or her
possessions; and the materialism which tethers our hearts to the earth.
In other words, to store up treasure on earth does not mean being
provident (making sensible provision for the future) but being *covetous* (like misers who hoard and materialists who always want more).
This is the real snare of which Jesus warns here.
Question 3. What are "treasures in heaven"? Jesus does not explain.
Yet surely we may say that to "store up" treasures in heaven is to do
anything on earth whose effects last for eternity. Encourage the group
to think of several examples.
Question 4. Not infrequently in Scripture the "eye" is equivalent to
the "heart." That is, to "set the heart" and to "fix the eye" on something
are synonyms. Therefore, Jesus' argument seems to go like this: just
as our eye affects our whole body, so our ambition (where we fix our
eyes and heart) affects our whole life.
Question 5. A supervisor usually only places limited demands on the
employee (for example, to work a certain number of hours a week).
Thus a person could satisfy two bosses if the hours required by each
do not conflict. But Jesus is referring to slave owners who own "all"
of a slave. Thus it is impossible to be owned completely by two masters.
Question 6. It is a pity that this passage is often read on its own,
isolated from what has gone before. Then the significance of the in-

troductory "Therefore I tell you" (v. 25) is missed. So we must relate this "therefore," this conclusion of Jesus, to the teaching which has led up to it. He calls us to thought before he calls us to action. He invites us to look clearly and coolly at the alternatives before us and to weigh them carefully. Only when we have grasped with our minds the comparative durability of the two treasures, the comparative usefulness of the two eye conditions and the comparative worth of the two masters, are we ready to consider Jesus' words: "Therefore I tell you" this is how you must go on to behave.

Questions 7-9. The Lord promises that our heavenly Father can be trusted to feed and clothe us. Yet even faithful believers are not exempt from the following: First, believers are not exempt from earning their own living. We cannot sit back in an armchair, twiddle our thumbs, mutter "my heavenly Father will provide" and do nothing. We have to work. As Paul put it later: "If a man will not work, he shall not eat" (2 Thess 3:10). Second, believers are not exempt from responsibility for others. It seems significant that in this same Gospel of Matthew the Jesus who says that our heavenly Father feeds and clothes his children later says that *we* must ourselves feed the hungry and clothe the naked, and will be judged accordingly (Mt 25:31-46). Third, believers are not exempt from experiencing trouble. Jesus forbids his people to worry. But freedom from *worry* and freedom from *trouble* are not the same thing. At the end of this paragraph the reason Jesus gives why we are not to *worry about tomorrow* is: "Each day has enough trouble of its own." So then God's children are promised freedom neither from work, nor from responsibility, nor from trouble, but only from worry. Worry is incompatible with Christian faith.

Study 11. A Christian's Relationships: Within God's Family. Matthew 7:1-12.
Purpose: To describe the quality of relationships the Father desires for his children.
Question 3. The picture of somebody struggling with the delicate operation of removing a speck of dirt from a friend's eye, while a vast

plank in his own eye entirely obscures his vision, is ludicrous. Yet when the caricature is transferred to ourselves and our ridiculous fault-finding, we do not always appreciate the joke. We have a fatal tendency to exaggerate the faults of others and minimize the gravity of our own. **Question 4.** The context does not refer to judges in courts of law but rather to the responsibility of individuals to one another. Likewise, our Lord's injunction to "judge not" cannot be understood as a command to suspend our critical faculties in relation to other people, to turn a blind eye to their faults (pretending not to notice them), to eschew all criticism and to refuse to discern between truth and error, goodness and evil. Much of Christ's teaching in the Sermon on the Mount is based on the assumption that we will (indeed should) make value judgments.

If, then, Jesus was neither abolishing law courts nor forbidding criticism, what did he mean by "Do not judge"? It is not a requirement to be blind, but rather a plea to be generous. Jesus does not tell us to cease to be human (by suspending our critical powers which help to distinguish us from animals) but to renounce the presumptuous ambition to be God (by setting ourselves up as judges).

Question 5. Again, it is evident that Jesus is not condemning criticism as such, but rather the criticism of others when we exercise no comparable self-criticism; nor correction as such, but rather the correction of others when we have not first corrected ourselves.

Question 6. By giving them these names, Jesus is indicating not only that they are more animals than humans, but that they are animals with dirty habits as well. The dogs he had in mind were not the well-behaved lapdogs of an elegant home but the wild pariah dogs, vagabonds and mongrels, which scavenged in the city's rubbish dumps. And pigs were unclean animals to the Jew, not to mention their love for mud. The apostle Peter was later to refer to them by bringing together two proverbs: "A dog returns to its vomit" and "A sow that is washed goes back to her wallowing in the mud" (2 Pet 2:22). So then the "dogs" and "pigs" with whom we are forbidden to share the gospel pearl are not just unbelievers. They must rather be those who have had ample opportunity to hear and receive the good news, but have decisively—even defiantly—rejected it. We cheapen God's gospel by letting them trample it under foot. At the same time, to give people up is a very serious step to take.

Question 7. All three verbs are present imperatives and indicate the persistence with which we should make our requests known to God. The force of Jesus' parable (vv. 9-11) lies in a contrast rather than a comparison between God and men. It is another *a fortiori* or "how much more" argument: if human parents (although evil) know how to give good gifts to their children, how much more will our heavenly Father (who is not evil but wholly good) *give good gifts to those who ask him* (v. 11).

Question 8. Not doing hateful acts is one thing (the Talmud and Confucius). Positively seeking someone's good is another (Jesus). Self-advantage often guides us in our own affairs; now we must also let it guide us in our behavior to others. All we have to do is use our imagination, put ourselves in the other person's shoes and ask, "How would I like to be treated in that situation?"

If someone asks about the Talmud, you can tell them that it is a collection of ancient rabbinic writings that form the basis of religious authority for traditional Judaism.

Study 12. A Christian's Relationships: To False Prophets. Matthew 7:13-20.
Purpose: To see the importance of entering the narrow gate and of watching out for those who teach otherwise.

Question 2. This is a simple observation question, so feel free to move quickly to the next question after people have had a chance to answer.

What is immediately striking about these verses is the absolute nature of the choice before us. We would all prefer to be given many more choices than only one, or better still to fuse them all into a conglomerate religion, thus eliminating the need for any choice. But Jesus cuts across our easygoing syncretism. He will not allow us the comfortable solutions we propose. Instead he insists that ultimately there is only one choice, because there are only two possibilities to choose from. There are two gates, two roads, two destinations and two groups. We must choose one or the other; we cannot be neutral.

Question 3. The narrowness of the road is due to divine revelation which restricts pilgrims to the confines of what God has revealed in Scripture to be true and good. Revealed truth imposes a limitation on what Christians may believe, and revealed goodness on how we may behave.

Questions 5 and 7. False prophets are adept at blurring the issue of salvation. Some so muddle or distort the gospel that they make it hard for seekers to find the narrow gate. Others try to make out that the narrow way is in reality much broader than Jesus implied, and that to walk it requires little if any restriction on one's belief or behavior. Yet others, perhaps the most pernicious of all, dare to contradict Jesus and to assert that the broad road does not lead to destruction, but that, as a matter of fact, all roads lead to God, and that even the broad and narrow roads, although they lead off in opposite directions, ultimately both end in life. No wonder Jesus likened such false teachers to *ferocious wolves*. They are responsible for leading people to the very destruction which they say does not exist.

Question 8. A prophet's "fruit" is not only his character and manner of life. Indeed, interpreters "who confine them to the life are, in my opinion, mistaken," wrote Calvin. A second fruit is the person's actual teaching. This is strongly suggested by the other use Jesus made of the same fruit-tree metaphor: "A tree is recognized by its fruit. You brood of vipers, how can you who are evil say anything good? For out of the overflow of the heart the mouth speaks. The good man brings good things out of the good stored up in him, and the evil man brings evil things out of the evil stored up in him" (Mt 12:33-35). So then, if a person's heart is revealed in his words, as a tree is known by its fruit, we have a responsibility to test a teacher by his teaching.

Question 9. The application of the "fruit" test is not altogether simple or straightforward. For fruit takes time to grow and ripen. We have to wait for it patiently. We also need an opportunity to examine it closely, for it is not always possible to recognize a tree and its fruit from a distance. Indeed, even at close quarters we may at first miss the symptoms of disease in the tree or the presence of a maggot in the fruit. To apply this to a teacher, what is needed is not a superficial estimate of his standing in the church, but a close and critical scrutiny of his character, conduct, message, motives and influence.

Study 13. A Christian's Commitment. Matthew 7:21-29.
Purpose: To decide on which foundation we are going to build our lives.
Question 2. The two final paragraphs of the Sermon are very similar. Both contrast the wrong and the right responses to Christ's teaching. Both show that neutrality is impossible and that a definite decision has to be made. Both stress that nothing can take the place of an active, practical obedience. And both teach that the issue of life and death on the Day of Judgment will be determined by our moral response to Christ and his teaching in this life. The only difference between the paragraphs is that, in the first, people offer a profession of their lips as an alternative to obedience and, in the second, a hearing with their ears.
Question 3. Jesus is not, of course, teaching that the way of salvation, or the way to enter "the kingdom of heaven" (v. 21) is by good works of obedience. For the whole New Testament offers salvation only by the sheer grace of God through faith. What Jesus is stressing, however, is that those who truly hear the gospel and profess faith will always obey him, expressing their faith in their works.
Question 4. A casual observer would not have noticed any difference between the two houses. For the difference was in the foundations, and foundations are not seen.
Questions 6-7. The real question is not whether we *hear* Christ's teaching (nor even whether we respect or believe it), but whether we *do* what we hear. Only a storm will reveal the truth. Sometimes a storm of crisis or calamity betrays what manner of person we are, for "true

piety is not fully distinguished from its counterfeit till it comes to the trial" (Bruce, *Synoptic Gospels*, p. 135). If not, the storm of the Day of Judgment will certainly do so.

Question 8. Jesus' hearers naturally compared and contrasted him with the many other teachers with whom they were familiar, especially the scribes. What struck them most was that he taught them "as one who had authority, and not as their teachers of the law." For the teachers of the law claimed no authority of their own. They conceived their duty in terms of faithfulness to the tradition they had received. So they delved into commentaries, searching for precedents, claiming the support of famous names among the rabbis. Their only authority lay in the authorities they were constantly quoting. Jesus, on the other hand, had not received a scribal education, scandalized the establishment by sweeping away the traditions of the elders, had no particular reverence for social conventions, and spoke with a freshness of his own which captivated some and infuriated others. A. B. Bruce summed up the difference by saying that the scribes spoke *"by* authority," while Jesus spoke *"with* authority" *(Synoptic Gospels,* p. 136).

If he did not teach like the teachers of the law, he did not teach like the Old Testament prophets either. The most common formula with which the prophets introduced their oracles, namely, "Thus says the Lord," is one Jesus never used. Instead, he would begin, "Truly, truly, I say to you," thus daring to speak in his own name and with his own authority, which he knew to be identical with the Father's.